# Proceedings of the Prayer Meeting

## (Ru'idaad-e-Jalsa-e-Du'aa)

*Held under the auspices of*

# Hazrat Mirza Ghulam Ahmad

*The Promised Messiah and Mahdi[as],
Founder of the Ahmadiyya Muslim Community*

ISLAM INTERNATIONAL PUBLICATIONS LTD.

**Proceedings of the Prayer Meeting**
English translation of *Ru'idaad-e-Jalsa-e-Du'aa*
*held under the auspices of,*
Hazrat Mirza Ghulam Ahmad, the Promised Messiah and Mahdi[as],
Founder of the Ahmadiyya Muslim Community

First published in Urdu in Qadian, India, 1900
First English translation published in the UK, 2018

© Islam International Publications Ltd.

Published by
Islam International Publications Ltd.
Unit 3, Bourne Mill Business Park
Guildford Road
Farnham, Surrey GU9 9PS, UK

Printed in UK at
Raqeem Press
Farnham, Surrey, GU9 9PS

Cover design by Usman Nasir Choudhary

For further information please visit www.alislam.org

ISBN 978-1-84880-904-8
10 9 8 7 6 5 4 3 2 1

# CONTENTS

# ABOUT HAZRAT
# MIRZA GHULAM AHMAD<sup>AS</sup>

Hazrat Mirza Ghulam Ahmad[as] was born in 1835 in Qadian, India. From his very youth, he dedicated himself to prayer and the study of the Holy Quran and other scriptures. He was deeply pained to observe the plight of Islam, which was being attacked from all directions. In order to defend Islam and present its teachings in their pristine purity, he penned more than ninety books, thousands of letters, and participated in several high profile religious debates and discourses. He argued that Islam is a living faith, which can lead man to establish communion with God to achieve moral and spiritual perfection.

Hazrat Mirza Ghulam Ahmad[as] started experiencing divine dreams, visions, and revelations at a young age. In 1889, under divine command, he started accepting initiation into the Ahmadiyya Muslim Community. The divine revelations continued to increase and he was commanded by God to announce that God had appointed him as the Reformer of the Latter Days who was prophesied in various religions under different titles. He claimed to be the very Promised Messiah and Mahdi whose advent had been foretold by the Holy Prophet Muhammad[sa]. The Ahmadiyya Muslim Community is now established in more than 200 countries.

After his demise in 1908, the institution of *Khilafat* (successorship) was established to continue his mission and movement, in fulfilment of the prophecies made in the Holy Quran and by the Holy Prophet Muhammad[sa]. Hazrat Mirza Masroor Ahmad[aba] is the Fifth Successor to the Promised Messiah[as] and the present Head of the Ahmadiyya Muslim Community.

# FOREWORD

On 2 February 1900, the day of Eidul-Fitr, a general meeting was held under the auspices of the Promised Messiah[as] to pray for the victory of the British Government in the ongoing war in Transvaal. This booklet records the proceedings of that meeting, known as *Jalsa-e-Du'aa*, or 'Prayer Meeting'.

This booklet includes the sermon delivered by the Promised Messiah[as] after the Eidul-Fitr prayers in which he gave an eloquent exegesis of *Surah an-Nas* (Holy Quran 114:1–7) and pointed out that the functions of *Ruboobiyyat* [Providence] and *Maalikiyyat* [Kingship] ultimately belong to Allah alone. But Allah the Exalted has created agencies within the world to exercise His *Ruboobiyyat* and *Maalikiyyat*. This is why due reverence to parents and those in authority, who faithfully execute their duties with justice, is enjoined on Muslims and represents an integral part of the Islamic faith.

This booklet also includes an Announcement in which an appeal was made for donations to aid the wounded in the Transvaal War, also known as the Second Boer War (1899–1902).

When 500 rupees were collected they were submitted to the respective authorities. Letters of appreciation from the authorities are also attached.

The booklet was translated from its original Urdu into English by Zulqarnain Bhirwana with assistance from Sayyed Tanwir Mujtaba. It was reviewed by al-Haaj Munawar Ahmed Saeed, Naser-ud-Din Shams, Abdul Wahab Mirza, and Hassan Faiyaz Khan. May Allah reward them all. Aameen.

**al-Haaj Munir-ud-Din Shams**
Additional Wakilut-Tasneef,
February 2018

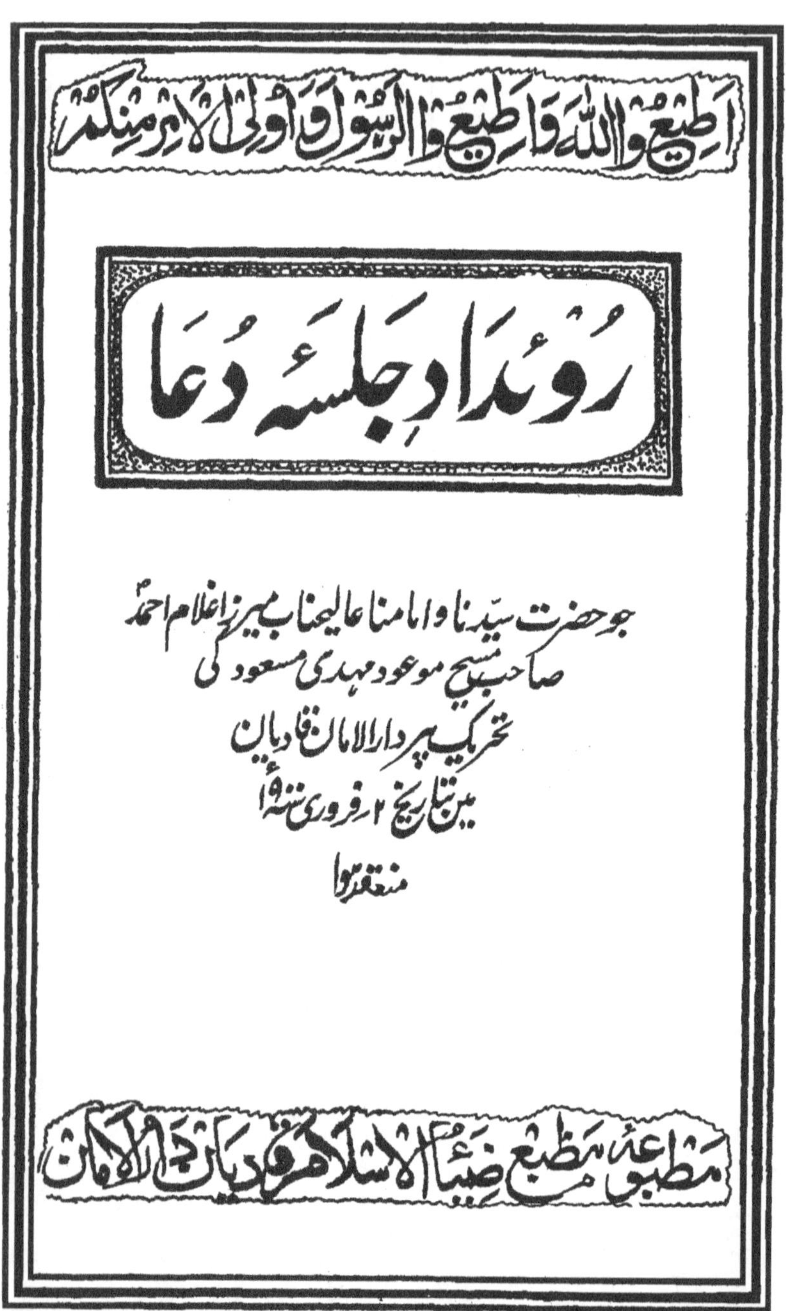

Facsimile of the original Urdu title page for *Ru'idaad-e-Jalsa-e-Du'aa*, printed in 1900.

*Obey Allah and obey His Messenger
and those in authority among you.*

## Proceedings of the Prayer Meeting

*which was held as adjured by our Master and Imam,
His Holiness Mirza Ghulam Ahmad[as], the
Promised Messiah and Mahdi, on
2 February 1900, in the
Abode of Peace,
Qadian.*

Published at:
ZIA-UL-ISLAM PRESS,
QADIAN—THE ABODE OF PEACE

Translation of the original Urdu title page for *Ru'idaad-e-Jalsa-e-Du'aa*.

بِسْمِ اللّٰهِ الرَّحْمٰنِ الرَّحِيْمِ [1]

نَحْمَدُهٗ وَ نُصَلِّیْ عَلٰی رَسُوْلِهِ الْكَرِيْمِ [2]

# *Proceedings of the Prayer Meeting*

*Held as adjured by His Holiness Mirza Ghulam Ahmad, the Promised Messiah[as] on 2 February 1900, in the Abode of Peace, Qadian*

# [INTRODUCTION]

Before presenting the proceedings to the readers it seems pertinent to state that the Imam of the Righteous, the Proof of Allah on Earth, and the Messiah of the Age—His Holiness, the Chief of Qadian, Mirza Ghulam Ahmad—is truly loyal to, and a well-wisher of, the present Government just as he is a well-wisher of all creation. His blessed person has spelled out the rights of the subjects and those of the Government as clearly as broad daylight.

---

1. In the name of Allah, the Gracious, the Merciful. [Publisher]

2. We praise Him and invoke His blessings upon His Noble Messenger. [Publisher]

He has so effectively and in diverse ways impressed the favours of this kind Government upon the hearts of his followers that the stain of hypocrisy with regard to this Empire has been altogether washed away from the hearts of this pure Jama'at. It is this hypocrisy which is seeping through the very fibre of poor, naïve, uninformed Muslims on account of their association with ignorant and bigoted mullahs. On the other hand, his followers have become as sincerely loyal and grateful to the British Government as they would have been to any Islamic one.

The Government is not unaware of the fact that the family of His Holiness has ever remained loyal and devoted to it and has always served it beyond their means in every difficult situation. The government officials can conclude therefrom that the family of Mirza Sahib had previously established ties of solidarity with the Government. While the ancestors of His Holiness supported the Government with troops and cavalry, His Holiness does his best, in his own way, to help it with a host of his heartfelt prayers. Every time there was a skirmish or battle on the Afghan frontier, or in Baluchistan or Burma, he continued to pray. He also celebrated the Diamond Jubilee of Her Majesty the Queen [of England] and the Empress [of India] and held a meeting wherein he prayed to God for her long life and success. Considering his life-style, which is strictly austere and has always been characterized by seclusion and solitude, how could he help this kind and generous Government in any other way except through his prayers? On the present occasion, too, as the British Government is dealing with undeserved trouble from a nation, which is being secretly abetted by other nations, this well-wisher of the people thought it appropriate to pray for the victory of our Government.

So, on 1st February, before the members of his Jama'at who had come from Afghanistan, Iraq and from various places throughout India such as Madras, Kashmir, Shahjahanpur, Jammu, Mithra, Jhang, Multan, Patiala, Kapurthala, Malerkotla, Ludhiana, Shahpur, Sialkot, Gujrat, Lahore, Amritsar, Gurdaspur etc., **His Holiness** expressed his wish to pray on the Eid day for the victory of the British Government. Upon hearing this, everyone wholeheartedly approved of it.

Accordingly, at 8 am on Eid day, accompanied by his followers, the Promised Messiah, may peace be upon him, made his way to a spacious ground situated to the west of Qadian, which has long since served as the *Eidgah* [Eid prayer site]. People from surrounding villages too had gathered there by 9 am. Then, Hazrat Maulaanaa Nur-ud-Din—**the Peerless Scholar of the Age**—led the **Eidul-Fitr** Prayer. After the prayer, the **Imam of the Age** stood up and delivered an eloquent **sermon.** His address was so engaging that all those present, numbering no less than one thousand, were completely spellbound. Moreover, it was very straightforward and intelligible—so much so that even the villagers, whose knowledge and understanding is somewhat superficial, were so impressed that they exclaimed, 'His Holiness speaks the truth!' As the original text would reveal, this address clearly portrays the rights of Allah as well as those of worldly rulers, and enlightens the public about the manifold favours of the British Government on the Muslims, and stresses the fact that Muslims are strictly bound by the Holy Quran to be loyal and devoted to the Government. Is there anyone in the world who can thus establish with sincerity and devotion the rights of the British Government from a religious perspective? It fell upon this champion to inspire true love for this Government within the hearts of his followers and to repeatedly emphasize, in both writing and speech, that if any of his followers were guilty of so much as the slightest duplicity towards this Government, he would not be considered a member of his Jama'at [Community] and would be disobedient to God and the Holy Prophet[sa]. This is because our appreciation of the British Government is not motivated by personal gain or selfish interest; rather, we are enjoined by Islam to express our sincere and heartfelt loyalty, in both word and deed. We hold it unlawful to indulge in hypocritical intrigues or to curry favour in order to acquire any title, property, or estate. Nothing more needs to be said as the address is given below word for word.

# THE SERMON



Muslims should be immensely grateful to Almighty Allah who has blessed them with a religion which is free from every kind of corruption, abomination, and defect in both theory and practice.

If man were to ponder carefully, he would realize that, in actual fact, all praiseworthy qualities and attributes belong to Almighty Allah, and that no human being or any other creature, in its own right, truly deserves praise and exaltation. Even with a little pondering, it would become quite obvious to him that whenever someone merited praise it was the result of creating something at a time when there was neither any existence nor any knowledge thereof; or providing all such means for life at a time when there was neither life nor knowledge of any such means for its survival, sustenance, and preservation; or showing mercy and protecting man at a time when many misfortunes could have befallen him. Or, someone might be worthy of praise for refusing to allow a diligent worker's labour to go to waste and granting due rights to those who work diligently. Even though rendering the worker his rights is apparently his due, someone may be laudable simply for the complete fulfilment of those rights.

These are the excellent qualities that can render someone worthy of praise and admiration. Reflect and see that all these praiseworthy qualities truly belong to Almighty Allah who perfectly exemplifies them to the exclusion of all others.

**First**, consider the attribute of creation and sustenance. In connection with this attribute, one can presume that parents and other benefactors have certain interests and motives for showing kindness. The proof thereof is that parents, for instance, feel happy when the child is born healthy, strong, and handsome. If it is a boy, this happiness increases manifold and celebrations are held, but if it is a girl, the entire household goes into mourning as if it were a dark day and they feel too embarrassed to go out in public. There are instances when some ignorant people put baby girls to death by using various devices, or pay little regard to their upbringing. And if the child is born crippled, blind, or handicapped, the parents desire its death and it would be no surprise if they were to kill it, believing it to be an unbearable burden. I have read that the Greeks used to intentionally kill such children. In fact their royal law prescribed that if a child was born disabled, handicapped, or blind, it should immediately be put to death.

This clearly illustrates that human thought is tainted with personal and selfish motives when it comes to upbringing and care. On the contrary, Almighty Allah has no personal motive in the creation and sustenance of His creatures (which are beyond imagination and description and which fill the heavens and the earth). Unlike the parents, He does not seek any service or provision [in return]. He creates them merely out of the decree of His Providence. Everyone will admit that planting a tree, watering it, taking care of it, and protecting it until it bears fruit, is indeed a great favour. So, if you reflect upon man and his condition and his sustenance, you will realize that God Almighty has bestowed a mighty favour by helping him through diverse upheavals, vicissitudes, and turns of fortune.

The **second** aspect is the one I have mentioned above; namely, the complete provision of means for the proper functionality of civilized life and human faculties prior to our creation. Look at all of the means that were provided for us even before we were born. Would we be able to see without the bright shining sun that now rises, through which light disseminates all around? By what other means could we have derived the benefits and advantages associated with light? Eyesight would have been useless had there been no sun or moon, or any other source of light. While it is also true that eyes have an ability to see, it is of no use without external light. It is, therefore, a singular favour of God that He has already provided all the means essential for utilizing various faculties. And how merciful of Him to have bestowed such faculties [upon man] wherein He has placed the capacity which is necessary for the perfection of man and the accomplishment of his goals! Allah has endowed the brain, the nervous system, and the vascular system with such properties that, when they are put to use, they achieve perfection. Thus He has also provided therewith the means of perfecting these faculties. Thusly does the framework of the internal system function that every single faculty is in full accord with the aims and objectives that ensure man's well-being.

The very same order applies to the external system. Whatever kind of profession one may have, the raw materials and tools relevant to it are provided well before one's birth. For example, if a cobbler was not able to find leather and thread, how would he produce them in order to pursue his craft? Similarly, what would a tailor sew if there was no cloth? The same is the case with every individual. No matter how skilled and knowledgeable a physician is, what can he do if there are no medicines? He may write a prescription after much deliberation, but what would he do if there was no medicine available in the market? How gracious of God that He has bestowed knowledge on the one hand, and, on the other, He has produced different kinds of plants, minerals, and animals which are helpful to the sick, and has endowed them with a variety of properties that can meet the unforeseen needs in every age. In short, nothing that God Almighty has created is useless. It is documented in medical texts that if anyone is suffering from urinary retention, sometimes urination restarts by entering lice through the opening of the urethra. Can anyone surmise the extent to which man can benefit from the support of all these things? Absolutely not! On the contrary, it is beyond anyone's imagination.

Thereafter, the fourth point is the reward of labour, which also depends upon God's grace. For example, whatever toil and trouble a man may take to till the land, if the help of Almighty God is not with him, how can he bring home the harvest? It is through His sheer grace and bounty that every single thing occurs in its own time. Accordingly, the people would have well-nigh perished

during the recent drought had God not poured forth the rain out
of His own grace, and protected the life of a large population.

In short, first and foremost, it is God Almighty who, in His
own right, is fully and perfectly worthy of praise. No one else is
worthy of worship in his own right. If any one else deserves any
praise, it is only because of dependence upon Him. Moreover,
even this is the mercy of God Almighty that despite His being
the unrivalled One without partner, He allows some to share
His meritorious attributes in a dependent way as He says in the
following holy *surah:*

قُلْ اَعُوْذُ بِرَبِّ النَّاسِ ۙ مَلِكِ النَّاسِ ۙ اِلٰهِ النَّاسِ ۙ مِنْ شَرِّ الْوَسْوَاسِ ۙ
الْخَنَّاسِ ۙ الَّذِىْ يُوَسْوِسُ فِىْ صُدُوْرِ النَّاسِ ۙ مِنَ الْجِنَّةِ وَ النَّاسِ ۝[1]

Herein, Almighty Allah has—along with the Truly Worthy
of praise [i.e. Himself]—implicitly indicated those also who
deserve praise temporarily; and this is so that high morals might
be perfected. Accordingly, He has specified three kinds of rights
in this *surah.* First, it exhorts to seek refuge with Allah, who
comprehends all perfect attributes, and is the Lord of mankind,
the King, and the Truly Worshipped and Sought One. This
*surah* is such that while firmly retaining the essence of *Tauheed*
[Oneness of God], it has simultaneously alluded to not violating
the rights of other people who manifest these titles in the manner of a shadow. Within the word *Rabb* is the indication that

---

1. *Surah an-Nas,* 114:2-7 [Publisher]

although it is God who actually nurtures and brings everything to perfection, there are also two other beings who temporarily and reflectively manifest [this] Nurturing Lordship [of God]; one physically and the other spiritually. The physical [manifestation] are parents and the spiritual [manifestation] is a religious head and spiritual guide.

It is mentioned in another place along with its explanation :

$$\text{وَقَضٰى رَبُّكَ اَلَّا تَعْبُدُوٓا اِلَّآ اِيَّاهُ وَ بِالْوَالِدَيْنِ اِحْسَانًا}^1$$

Meaning that, God has decreed that we should worship none other than Him and be benevolent to our parents. Indeed, how marvellous this *ruboobiyyat* [providence] is that when man is an infant and is completely helpless, what diverse services the mother performs in such a precarious condition, and how the father, in these circumstances, becomes the supporter of the mother's efforts. God Almighty, in His sheer grace, has created these two agents to take care of the helpless creatures and has bestowed upon them a reflection of the light of His love. It should, however, be borne in mind that the love of parents is adventitious while the love of God Almighty is inherent reality, and unless it is inspired into the hearts by God, no human being—be they a friend, a peer, or a ruler—can ever love anyone. This is the mystery of the perfect *Ruboobiyyat* of God that the parents bear such love for their children that, in raising them, they cheerfully endure all kinds of troubles so much so they do not even hesitate to die to protect their lives.

---

1. *Surah Bani Israa'eel,* 17:24 [Publisher]

Hence, for the perfection of high morals, God Almighty has alluded to parents and spiritual guides in the expression **Rabbin-Naas** so that out of gratitude for this reflective and manifest design, one may be moved to express gratitude to the True Sustainer and Guide.

The key to unravelling this mystery is that this noble *surah* begins with stating **Rabbin-Naas** rather than beginning with **Ilaahin-Naas**. Since the spiritual guide instructs in accordance with the will of God Almighty as well as with His providence and guidance, he too is included herein. The second verse is **Malikin-Naas**; meaning, seek refuge with Allah who is your King. This is one more point of guidance aimed at acquainting people with the principles of the civilized world and making them cultured. In reality, Almighty Allah alone is the King. However, there is an indication in this that there do exist kings by way of reflection and this is the very reason why it also contains reference to fulfilling the rights of the reigning king of the time.

There is no qualification here whatsoever—be the king an infidel, a pagan, or a monotheist— rather, it is a general reference regardless of whatever religion the king be; religion and belief are dealt elsewhere. Wherever God speaks of a benefactor in the Holy Quran, He imposes no such condition that he be a Muslim, a monotheist, or a follower of a particular sect; rather, the benefactor is spoken of in general terms to whatever religion he may belong. God Almighty strictly admonishes us in His own Holy Word to be good to the one who is good, as the following verse makes very clear:

هَلْ جَزَآءُ الْاِحْسَانِ اِلَّا الْاِحْسَانُ <sup>1</sup>

Can the reward of goodness be anything but goodness?

**I now announce to my Jama'at** and to the entire audience clearly and with great transparency that **the British Government** is our benefactor which has conferred great favours upon us. Anyone whose age is sixty or seventy years is well aware of how we endured life during the days of **Sikh** rule. The many hardships faced by the Muslims in those days are no secret; their recollection makes the body shudder and the heart tremble. During that period Muslims were prohibited from performing acts of worship and other religious obligations, the observance of which being dearer to them than their own lives. *Azan,* which is prologue to Prayer, was forbidden to be sounded aloud. If ever a *muazzin*[2] would mistakenly call out *Allah-o-Akbar* [Allah is the Greatest] aloud, he would be killed. Likewise, the matter of what is lawful and unlawful in Islam was needlessly interfered with. Once, in a case involving a cow [and its alleged slaughter], five thousand helpless Muslims were put to death. In Batala it so happened that a Sayyed, a resident thereof, on returning home, found a herd of cows crowding his doorstep. He slightly pushed them with the tip of his sword and inadvertently pierced the skin of a cow. Upon this event, the poor fellow was apprehended and it was vociferously proposed that he be executed. In the end, his life was spared after many solicitations, but his hand was chopped off.

---

1. *Surah ar-Rahmaan,* 55:61 [Publisher]

2. A person who calls the *azan* at the appointed times of Prayers. [Publisher]

Now, in contrast, look at the extent of freedom enjoyed by the people of every caste and creed.

Let us confine ourselves to just the Muslims. The **Empire** allows full freedom to perform religious obligations and acts of worship. It does not unjustly interfere with the property, life, and honour of someone, in sharp contrast to those turbulent times when everyone—no matter how blameless his conduct—feared for his life and property. However, if someone is guilty of evil conduct, thus becoming liable to punishment on account of his perversity, crookedness, and perpetration of crimes, that is quite a separate issue. Or, if one is lax in worship due to his own mis-belief and negligence, it is a different matter altogether, for the Government has granted complete freedom in every respect. At present, you can become as ardent a worshipper as you wish because there is no restriction whatsoever. The Government itself preserves the sanctity of religious places of worship and expends thousands of rupees on their maintenance; whereas, against this, during Sikh rule, the environment was such that mosques were converted into places where bhang [hemp leaves] drink was pre-pared and horses were stabled, an example of which is present here in **Qadian,** while the major towns of the Punjab abound in such instances. In Lahore, several mosques are in the posses-sion of the Sikhs to this day. But now, in opposition to this, the British Government pays every kind of due respect to these holy places and considers it among its duties to honour and revere all religious buildings, just as His Excellency the Right Honourable Viceroy, Lord **Curzon** recently demonstrated through his own example by not wearing shoes when entering the central mosque of Delhi; thus, he set a commendable example of high moral qualities worthy of royalty. It is evident from his speeches that he has delivered from time to time on various occasions that he accords particular respect to religious buildings. Moreover, note that the Government has not made any announcements against sounding the call to prayer or against fasting; rather, they ensure the provision of every kind of food of which not even a trace existed in the wretched reign of the Sikhs. Every kind of dietary item has been supplied—ice, soda water, biscuits, bread, etc.—and every kind of facility has been provided. This is an incidental help which they have extended to our **Islamic practices.** Now, should someone refuse to fast of their own accord, this is a different issue. It is a matter of pity that the Muslims themselves are being disrespectful to the Shariah. For example, look at those who fasted in these days, they have not become any thinner, and those who passed this month with little regard for its obligations have not become any fatter. Time passed for them both. They were winter fasts; there was only one change in the meal timings to eat at 4 or 5 o'clock [in the morning] instead of eating at 7 or 8 o'clock [in the morning]. Despite such convenience, many people did not honour the sanctity [of Ramadan] granted to it by Allah and treated this **honourable** guest of God Almighty—the **month of Ramadan**—with great contempt. The coming of Ramadan during the months of so much ease [to fast] was a kind of gauge, and these fasts served as the scales to distinguish the obedient from the sinful. By the grace of God Almighty, the Government has allowed freedom of every kind. A variety of fruits and other edibles are readily available, and there is no comfort and convenience that cannot be accessed today. Despite all this, what is the reason behind this negligence that we witness? Only that hearts are no longer steeped in faith. Sadly, God is not even given the same regard as a lowly sweeper, as if they think there will never be any accountability before God or any obligation to Him, and as if there will be no summoning before His Judgment Seat. If only the disbelievers would ponder and reflect over the proof of the existence of God Almighty that shines brighter than millions of suns! It is an occasion for pity that upon seeing a shoe it is understood with full certainty that it has a maker, but how unfortunate it is that even upon observing the endless creation of God Almighty they either do not believe in Him or their belief amounts to nothing. Indeed, God Almighty has conferred many favours upon us, one of which is that He has delivered us out of a burning oven. The Sikh rule was like a blazing oven, while the **advance of the British** is an advance of grace and blessing. I have heard that when the very first of the first British arrived, a *muazzin* in Hoshiarpur called the *azan* [formal call for Islamic daily Prayers] out loudly. Since it was still the beginning, the Hindus and Sikhs thought that the British would also prohibit the loud call of the *azan*, or, like them, would cut off the hands of someone who had injured a cow; therefore, they apprehended the *muazzin* who called out the loud *azan*. They formed a large mob and took him to the Deputy Commissioner. Eminent Hindu chiefs and money lenders gathered together and complained: "Sir, our dough has been polluted and our utensils have been desecrated." When these statements were communicated to the British officer, he wondered if the call to prayer had such an effect as to render the food items unclean. He instructed the head clerk not to register the case without first verifying this. So, he ordered the *muazzin* to once again sound the call to prayer. The *muazzin* was fearful that this might be regarded as the second offence, so he hesitated to make the call. However, when he was assured to the contrary, he made the call to prayer as loud as before. The honourable officer, upon this, said it did him no harm and inquired from the head clerk if any harm had been done to him. He too said that, in fact, no harm had been caused. At last, the *muazzin* was released and permitted to make the call to prayer as he liked. ***Allah-o-Akbar*** [Allah is the Greatest]! How much freedom indeed and how great a favour of Almighty Allah! Upon such manifest grace and favour, if one's heart cannot feel the kindness of the English Government, that heart is ungrateful and disloyal and is worthy of being ripped out of the chest.

In this village of ours, too, at a place where our mosque is located, there used to be a piece of land allotted to state officials. Those were my childhood days but I have heard from credible men that when the British arrived here the same old laws remained in effect for a few days. During those days an official came here. He was accompanied by a Muslim soldier who came into the mosque and told the *muazzin* to sound the call to prayer. The *muazzin* fearfully called the *azan* in a low tone as he used to. The soldier asked him if that was the way he normally sounded the call to prayer. The *muazzin* replied, 'Yes, this is the way we do it.' The soldier insisted, 'No, climb the roof and sound the *azan* out loud, and make the call to prayer as loud as you possibly can.' The *muazzin* was initially fearful, but finally, at the insistence of the soldier, he sounded the call to prayer out loud. At this, all the Hindus rallied together and apprehended the mullah. The poor fellow became fearful and worried that the official might hang him. The soldier assured him that he was with him. At last, the brutal and heartless Brahmans took the mullah to the official and complained: 'Sir, he has defiled us.' The official was aware that the government had changed and the old **Sikh Regime** no longer existed. Yet, he asked politely, 'Why did you make the call to prayer out loud?' The soldier stepped forward and said, 'It was not he, but I who made the call to prayer.' The official said [addressing the crowd], 'Wretches! Why do you raise an uproar? Cows are now openly slaughtered in Lahore without any restriction, and here you are fretting over the *azan*. Go quietly and hold your peace.'

In short, the sincere truth that proceeds from our heart is that it would be utterly ungrateful and disloyal on our part if we did not acknowledge the favour of a people who have lifted us from the depths of oppression.

Aside from this, great ignorance ran rampant in the Punjab. An old man, Kammay Shah, narrates that he had seen his mentor pray fervently to be able to see *Sahih al-Bukhari* even if for once. At times, thinking how impossible it was to have a look at it, he cried so much during the prayer that he almost choked on it. Now, that very *Bukhari* is available in Amritsar and Lahore for two to four rupees. There used to be one *maulawi* **Sher Muhammad** who somewhere happened upon a few pages of **Ihyaa-ul-Uloom.** For a long time he would show them with great delight and pride to the worshippers after each prayer, saying, 'Look, this is *Ihyaa-ul-Uloom.*' He was so anxious to get a hold of the complete book from somewhere. *Ihyaa-ul-Uloom* is now available everywhere in published form. In short, through the blessing of the arrival of the British, the spiritual eye of the people has opened as well, and Almighty God is well aware of how much patronage was extended to religion through this Government which would not have even been possible in any other government. Through the blessing of the press and the production of different kinds of paper, all sorts of books can be purchased at a very low cost. Moreover, through the Post Office they are readily delivered to homes from various locations. Thus, the path to propagate the truths of religion has been made so clear and smooth.

Among all other blessings made accessible under this Government and which promote the cause of religion, one is the remarkable development of rational faculties and intellectual abilities. Since the Government allows every single sect the freedom to propagate its own religion, people have an ample opportunity to critically appraise and reflect on the principles and arguments of every religion. When the followers of different religions attacked Islam, it provided the followers of Islam with an occasion to reflect upon their own religious books for the corroboration and truth of their doctrine, and thus their faculty for reasoning was sharpened. It is obvious that just as physical strength improves with exercise, in the very same way spiritual faculties grow and thrive through discipline. Just as a horse is disciplined by a nimble rider, so has the coming of the British provided an opportunity to delve into the fundamentals of religion, with the result that those who reflect and ponder have become more resolute and steadfast in their true faith. Wherever the opponents of the **Noble Quran** pointed their accusing finger, from that very place was discovered a concealed treasure of truth by those who reflect.

On account of this freedom, there has been considerable advancement even in the knowledge of the Word [of Allah]. And this advancement has specifically occurred over here. Now, should someone come from Turkey or Syria, he would not be able to sufficiently refute the objections raised by the Christians or the Aryas—regardless of however scholarly or proficient he may be—because he never had the opportunity to freely and extensively compare the principles of different religions. In short, just as there is worldly peace throughout the country under the British Government, so also is there a widespread prevalence of spiritual peace. Since I am concerned with religious and spiritual affairs, I will chiefly speak of those things that the Government has bestowed upon us as a favour, inasmuch as they help us carry out our religious duties.

It should be kept in mind that one can perform acts of worship with freedom and satisfaction only when **four preconditions** are met. They are as follows:

**FIRST IS HEALTH**—If a person is too weak to get up from bed, how can he observe fasts and Salat [Prayers]? Likewise, he would be unable to perform the Hajj, Zakat, and various other obligations. Now, it is worth noting how many means we have been provided by the Government for the maintenance of physical health. In every major city and town, there is at least one hospital where patients are treated with great care and sympathy. Furthermore, medicines, meals, etc. are provided for free. Some patients are admitted into the hospital and are looked after and cared for in such a way that it would be impossible for someone to be treated with such ease and comfort even in their own home. The Government has set up a separate department for healthcare on which millions of rupees are expended annually. It has taken extraordinary measures to keep towns and cities clean. There are systems for drainage and waste disposal. What is more, all sorts of effective medicines are manufactured and supplied at fairly low prices so that everyone can afford to keep certain medicines at home and take them when needed. By establishing large colleges, medical education has been abundantly disseminated to the extent that doctors are found even in the rural areas. To prevent certain dangerous diseases like smallpox, cholera, plague, etc.—especially with regard to the plague—all of the recently taken measures by the Government command our deepest gratitude.

To summarize, the Government has extended every kind of required assistance with respect to health, and has thereby provided great support toward fulfilling the first and foremost requirement of worship.

**SECOND PREREQUISITE IS FAITH**—If one loses faith in God Almighty and His commandments and is eaten away from within by faithlessness and impiety, one is unable to carry out divine injunctions. This is why so many people are fond of saying, ایہہ جگ مٹھا تے اگلا کن ڈٹھا ['Delightful indeed is this world; who has seen the next?']

It is a pity that a criminal can get hanged upon the testimony of two people, yet—despite the collective testimony of one hundred and twenty-four thousand **Messengers** and countless *auliyaa* [friends of Allah]—this kind of impiety has still not departed from the hearts of people. In every age, through His mighty **Signs and miracles,** God Almighty proclaims: أنا الموجود ['I am present'], yet these wretches, having ears, hear not. In short, this stipulation is also a vital condition. For this, too, we **ought to** be grateful to the **British** Government, because the strengthening of faith and belief requires general religious education which in turn depends upon the publication of religious books. All kinds of religious books are [now] available, thanks to the press and the post office. The newspapers also facilitate the exchange of views. Here is a major opportunity for the good-natured people to become firmly steeped in faith and belief.

In addition to the above, one thing that is most **important and crucial** for one to stand firm in faith is the **Divine Signs** that appear at the hands of a person who comes from God as [His] **appointee** and revives the lost truths and verities through his practical conduct. **So God should be thanked** who, in this age, **has commissioned such a person to revive faith** and sent him so that people may advance in their strength of conviction. He has appeared during the rule of this auspicious Government. Who is he? **He is the very one who stands in your midst, speaking these words.**

It is an unquestionable fact that unless man is perfect in faith he cannot perform good deeds to perfection. The more flawed or defective one's faith, the more lax and weak one will be in practice. This is why he alone is called *wali* [a friend of Allah] who is **perfect** in every aspect of [faith], is not defective in any respect, and whose acts of worship are performed with complete perfection. In short, the second condition is the soundness of faith.

**THIRD PREREQUISITE IS MAN'S FINANCIAL STRENGTH—** The construction of mosques and other such things affiliated with Islam rely upon financial strength. Without it, civic life and the management of affairs—especially those of mosques—would be very difficult..

Now take a look at the British Government from this perspective. The Government has encouraged every kind of trade. It has promoted education and given jobs to the locals, even assigning some to major posts, and by providing means of travel it has helped people earn money in other countries. See that there are people working as doctors, lawyers, court officials, clerks, and employees in the Education Department. In short, people are earning quite substantially from many different sources. Moreover, merchants trading in different kinds of goods who set off to England and other far-off countries like Africa, Australia, etc., come back wealthy and prosperous. To sum up, the Government has opened up opportunities to earn livelihood and has created a great many sources of income.

**FOURTH REQUISITE IS PEACE**—The fulfilment of the condition of peace does not lie within the power of an individual. Since the world was created, the achievement of this objective has been dependent upon the government. The more goodwill and sincerity the government has, the more will this requirement be met. The condition of peace is being perfectly fulfilled in this age. It is my firm conviction that the days during the Sikh regime were even worse than the nights of the British rule. There is a nearby village named Borh[1]. If some woman from here had to go that far, she would go crying and wondering whether she would be able to return at all; whereas, now, one can go to the ends of the country without facing any danger. The means of travel have been made so easy that every kind of comfort is now available—like sitting and sleeping in the train as if at home and going anywhere one pleases. An extensive Department of Police exists for the protection of

---

1. This village is located at a distance of 2 miles from Qadian. [Publisher]

property and life; courts are freely accessible for the protection of rights, and one may seek as much legal help as one likes.

How remarkable, indeed, are these favours that have ensured our practical freedom! Then surely, it is very surprising if in such an environment—wherein countless favours are being enjoyed by the body and soul—we do not develop within ourselves a sense of amicability and gratitude? One who is not grateful to God's creation cannot be grateful to God Almighty. Why so? Because that creation is an ambassador of God Himself and moves under the authority of the will of God alone.

In short, all these things that I have pointed out compel a good-hearted person to be grateful to such a benefactor. That is why I repeatedly speak of the favours of the British Government in my books and speeches, for my heart actually fills with joy at its favours. The ungrateful and ignorant people, by imputing their own hypocritical inclinations to me, regard this practice of mine—which is born out of honesty and sincerity—as sycophancy.

Now, reverting to the issue at hand, I would like to explain that, in this *surah,* God Almighty first stated رَبِّ النَّاس [*Rabbin-naas*—Lord of mankind], then ملك النَّاس [*Malikin-naas*—King of mankind]. In the end He stated إله النَّاس [*Ilaahin-naas*—the God of mankind], who is the One truly sought after and desired by man. The term إله [*Ilaah*] means 'One worthy of worship', 'the desired One', and 'the sought after'. The phrase لَا إله إلَّا الله [*La ilaaha illallah*] therefore means لَا مَعْبُوْدَ لِيْ وَ لَا مَقْصُوْدَ لِيْ وَ لَا مَطْلُوْبَ لِيْ إلَّا اللهُ ['I have no object of worship, no target, nor anything sought after, except Allah']. This alone is true *Tauheed* [the Oneness of Allah] that

Almighty Allah alone be considered worthy of every praise and exaltation. Then He says:

$$ \text{مِنْ شَرِّ الْوَسْوَاسِ الْخَنَّاسِ}^{1} $$

Meaning that, seek refuge from the evil of the whisper-dropping خنّاس [*khannaas*—the sneaking whisperer].

In Arabic the term *khannaas* means the serpent which is called نحاش in Hebrew in an allusion to the evil that it was guilty of, in the earlier days. Here the word *Iblees* or 'Satan' has not been used in order that man may recall his original trial whereby Satan had deceived his two ancestors. It was on that occasion that he was given the name *khannaas* [the evil whisperer].

God has chosen this sequence in order to warn man by reminding him of past events; namely that, just as Satan had tempted man to disobey God, so might he also—at any moment—tempt man to disobey and rebel against the ruler of the time. Thus, one must always keep an eye on the intentions and designs of one's ego and see how willing he is to submit to the authority of the ruler. Also, one should continue to strive and pray to God Almighty that Satan may not enter into him through any opening.

Now, the command in this *surah* is none other than the command to obey God Almighty alone, inasmuch as true obedience belongs to Him. However, the command for obedience to parents, the spiritual leader and guide, and the ruler of the time, has also been enjoined by God Himself. The reward of such obedience will be that you will break free from the grip of *khannaas*

---

1. *Surah an-Nas*, 114:5. [Publisher]

THE SERMON25

[the evil whisperer]. Therefore, seek refuge with Allah that you be protected against the evil of the inspiration cast by *khannaas*, insofar as a believer is not bitten by the same hole twice. Do not get caught again into that which has once brought affliction upon you. Therefore, there is a clear indication in this *surah* to obey the ruler of the time.

*Khannaas* [the evil whisperer] has been invested with qualities in the same way that God Almighty has placed certain qualities within wood, water, fire, and other objects and elements. As س and ص are interchangeable in Arabic, the word عنصر [*'ansar* meaning 'element'] is, in fact, عَنْ سِرّ, the meaning being: 'It is one of the divine mysteries at which point man's investigations actually come to a halt.' In short, everything is from God, whether it be of a simple nature or a complex one.

Given the fact that Allah, having sent such rulers, has delivered us from thousands of hardships and has brought about such a change as if, rescuing us from a burning pit, He placed us into a garden—wherein lie delightful plants and flowing streams in every direction, and wherein blow cool, pleasant breezes—how incredibly ungrateful would it be if one should overlook all His favours! Especially, the members of my Jama'at whom God has blessed with insight and who are truly free from hypocrisy—for the one with whom they have established a bond does not have so much as a trace of hypocrisy in him—should exemplify the highest paragon of gratitude. I am absolutely convinced that my Jama'at is free from hypocrisy, and, in establishing a bond with me, their intuitive perception did not err; for, in truth, I am the very one whose advent was bound to be accepted by those with faithful sagacity. God Almighty is Witness and is Fully Aware that I am the same **truthful, trustworthy, and promised one** whose **advent** was foretold by the blessed speech of our lord and master, the truthful and trustworthy Messenger, may peace and blessings of Allah be upon him. I say truly that those who have not established a bond with me are deprived of this blessing. *Firaasat* [good judgment and intuition] is something akin to a miracle. The word فراست [*firaasat/faraasat*] can be pronounced with the vowel sound 'a' with a *fathah* as well as 'i' with a *kasrah* in its first letter 'f'. When pronounced with the vowel sound 'a' with a *fathah* on the first letter 'f', it means the act of mounting a horse. A true believer mounts the horse of his self with intuitive discernment. He is granted light from God through which he finds his way. This is why the Messenger of Allah, may peace and blessing of Allah be upon him, said:

اتقوا فراسة المؤمن فانه ينظر بنور الله

Meaning that, beware of the intuition of a believer, for he sees by the light of Allah. In short, the great proof of the sound intuition of my Jama'at is that they have recognized the light of God. In this very manner, I entertain hope that the members of my Jama'at will improve their practical condition as well, since they are not hypocrites and are completely innocent of the conduct of our opponents who praise Government officials when meeting them yet denounce them as kafir upon returning home. Hearken, O my Jama'at! Remember that God does not approve of this conduct. You, who have associated yourselves with me only for the sake of God: **Do good to those who do good and forgive those who do evil.** A person cannot be truthful unless he be of one colour. One who proceeds in a hypocritical manner and adopts two colours is eventually exposed. There is a famous adage: دروغگورا حافظه نباشد ['A liar has no memory.']

**Now I wish to state another important point** which is that rulers often have to embark on military campaigns that also serve to protect and safeguard their subjects. As you have seen, **our Government** has had to fight wars on the [Afghan] Frontier on several occasions. Although the Frontier people are Muslims, in my opinion they are in the wrong. Their war against the British has no justification from any religious aspect or point of view, nor do they, in fact, fight for any religious motive. Can they dare offer the excuse that the Government has denied freedom to the Muslims?

The Government, truly, has allowed freedom the like of which cannot be found, even when living in Kabul or its suburbs. We have not heard the Amir spoken of in good terms either. Greed is the only motive for which these insane Frontiersmen are fighting. A petty sum like ten or twenty rupees is enough to dampen their warrior spirit. They are fanatics who spoil the good name of Islam. Islam establishes the rights of the ruler of the time and those of the benefactor, whereas these mean-spirited people transgress the limits of Allah for their selfish ends. The fact that they readily murder a human being for a piece of bread is a strong proof of their meanness, stupidity, and brutality.

Our Government is currently at war with a small republic, Transvaal, which is no bigger than the Punjab. It was an act of sheer folly on its part to have engaged in warfare with such a great empire. But now that the fighting has begun, it is incumbent upon every Muslim to pray for the victory of the British. As for Transvaal, what concern have we with it? Our duty is to wish well for one who has bestowed countless favours upon us. When a neighbour has so many rights that a heart bleeds upon hearing his suffering, does it not grieve our hearts upon reading the hardships endured by the loyal soldiers of the British Government? In my view, he indeed is dark-hearted who does not consider the Government's worries as his own. Remember, there are different kinds of leprosy; one affects the body, the other affects the soul on account of which one falls into the bad habit of delighting in the misfortunes of others and resenting their well-being.

There used to live a man in our marketplace. Every time someone faced a trial in court, he would go about asking as to how the case was proceeding. If he was told that the accused was acquitted or that the trial went well for the defence, he would stand aghast and fall silent. And if someone told him that the accused had been indicted, he would be overjoyed and would seat the man by his side and listen to the whole story. In short, certain people are so filled with malice that they are eager to hear bad news and revel in the misfortune of others, since they themselves are satanic in nature. Thus, it is improper to bear ill-will towards anyone, let alone someone who is benevolent.

I urge my Jama'at to avoid the example of such people and to pray with complete sympathy and genuine goodwill for the victory of the British Government, and to demonstrate their loyalty in practice as well. I do not make these statements with a view to currying favour or receiving some reward. What have I to do with favours, rewards, or worldly titles? The All-Knowing God is well aware of my intentions and knows that my actions are for His sake alone and are in conformity with His will. He has enjoined us to be grateful to our benefactor, and, by being grateful, we obey our Glorious Lord, expecting a reward from Him alone. Members of my Jama'at! I call upon you to hold your kind Government in great esteem.

Now, let us pray for Transvaal war.

T H E    E N D

Thereafter, His Holiness, with great earnestness and sincerity, raised his hands in prayer and all those present, exceeding one thousand in number, joined him in the prayer. They prayed at length for the triumph and victory [of the British Government]. Later, His Holiness suggested that a donation be raised for the wounded on the British side. An announcement was published in this regard. It was as given below.

The writer,
Mirza Khuda Bakhsh,
Qadian

# AN IMPORTANT ANNOUNCEMENT FOR MY JAMA'AT

بِسْمِ اللهِ الرَّحْمٰنِ الرَّحِيْمِ <sup>1</sup>

نَحْمَدُهٗ وَ نُصَلِّیْ عَلٰی رَسُوْلِهِ الْكَرِیْمِ <sup>2</sup>

Given the great favours of the British Government bestowed generally upon the Muslims of India and specifically upon the Muslims of the Punjab, whatever degree of gratitude Muslims express to this kind Government would still be far too little; for, Muslims have still not forgotten the time when they were suffering in a burning pit at the hands of the Sikhs whose tyranny not only destroyed their worldly status, but also the state of their religion to an even greater extent. Let alone the performance of religious obligations, some Muslims were put to death for saying *azan* and performing prayers. In such a lamentable plight, Allah Almighty sent from afar this blessed Government like a much needed cloud to liberate us, which not only came to deliver us from the claws of those tyrants, but also established permanent peace, provided every means of comfort, and allowed religious freedom to the extent that we can now freely propagate our mighty Faith in the best manner possible. On the occasion of Eidul-Fitr, I spoke

---

1. In the name of Allah, the Gracious, the Merciful. [Publisher]

2. We praise Him and invoke His blessings upon His Noble Messenger. [Publisher]

extensively on this subject which has been reported in brief by the English newspapers and soon my brother-in-faith Mirza Khuda Bakhsh will publish a detailed report on it. On this happy occasion of Eid, having mentioned the favours of the Government, I directed my Jama'at, who are truly loyal to the Government and consider it a heinous sin to live a life of hypocrisy as led by others, to earnestly pray for their benevolent Government that Almighty Allah may grant it a great victory in the ongoing war in Transvaal. I also pointed out that the foremost obligation in Islam, after the rights of Allah, is showing sympathy for people and that it is a rewarding deed, in particular, to show sympathy for the servants of such a kind Government that safeguards our lives, property, and, above all, our Faith. Hence, I urged the members of my Jama'at, no matter where they live, to make a monetary contribution within their means and resources for the wounded and maimed of the Transvaal War. The members of my Jama'at are hereby informed through this announcement that they should prepare a list of contributors in every town, collect the sums, and send them to Qadian before the 1st of March—care of Mirza Khuda Bakhsh, as he has been assigned this duty. After the receipt of money along with the lists, the final list of contributions will be recorded in the aforementioned report. My Jama'at should treat this task as urgent and carry it out without delay. **Peace be upon you.**

**Author,**
**Mirza Ghulam Ahmad of Qadian,**
10 February 1900

# A GLAD TIDING

*[Compiled by Mirza Khuda Baksh of Qadian]*

The Announcement of 10th February expressed the wish to publish the list of contributors along with the report. But since the report has already taken up so much space, His Holiness, the Guide of Mankind, does not deem it appropriate to publish the list. Only a few people have donated large sums, the rest being humble contributions. The largest amount is one hundred rupees donated by Nawab Muhammad Ali Khan, the Chief of Malerkotla, and the smallest is three pennies.

Since, His Holiness **the Promised Messiah, may peace and blessings be upon him,** does not approve of unreasonable delay in the dispatch of monetary contributions, after having waited for the date specified in the announcement, the amount of five hundred rupees was dispatched to the Chief Secretary of the Punjab Government. Now I intend to reproduce the receipt sent by the above British official, but, first, I deem it important to mention that His Holiness is very pleased with those who, in keeping with their means and position, have shown concern and donated for the wounded, the widowed, and the orphaned on the British side. I congratulate the ones who, by obeying the command of the true Imam, have not only pleased their spiritual guide but have also earned the pleasure of the true Lord of Sovereignty as well as the pleasure of worldly rulers. For, in the Holy Book of the Muslims, the Lord of heaven and earth has strictly enjoined us to fulfil the rights of men after fulfilling the rights of Allah, and has declared that sympathy for mankind leads to His pleasure and favour. He has commanded us to be compassionate towards all, regardless of their religion, race, or whether they be of the East or the West. In light of this, sympathy with our benefactor who protects our rights becomes all the more necessary. Can be there be any benefactor and well-wisher greater than this British Government that has helped the Muslims on a number of occasions and, having delivered them from gruelling hardships, provided them with a haven of peace and security?

The donation made by this poor Jama'at was too insignificant vis-a`-vis our great Government. Nevertheless, this generous Government accepted it with great respect and, moreover, expressed its pleasure over it. Fortunate are those who pay due regard to the prerequisites of subject-ruler relationship by sharing the joy and grief of the rulers of the time. And how generous and magnificent is the Government that regards humble donations and greetings of its subjects with such respect and honour! What can be more encouraging than the fact that His Excellency, the Lieutenant Governor, with all his titles, sent a receipt in appreciation of a paltry sum of five hundred rupees. Moreover, His Excellency, the Governor General, Viceroy, with all his titles, and the Lieutenant Governor of the Punjab expressed their pleasure and gratitude to His Holiness—the Noble Imam, the Guide of the People—for sending a congratulatory telegraph on the British victory in South Africa. So, this Government deserves our gratitude at all events. May God Almighty prolong the rule of this

Government, the champion of peace and freedom, and bestow upon it a fair share of the heavenly kingdom.

I now give below the three thanksgiving letters for the pleasure of our readers.

*Letter Number 234*[1]

*FROM:*

*J.M.C Douie I.C.S, Acting Chief Secretary,*
  *Government of the Punjab*

*TO:*

*Mirza Ghulam Ahmad Sahib, Chief of Qadian,*
*District Gurdaspur, dated 26<sup>th</sup> March, Lahore*

Dear Sir! His Excellency Lieutenant-Governor has instructed us to inform you that the generous donation of Rupees 500 sent by you and your followers for the welfare of the British wounded and sick in South Africa has been received and forwarded to Messrs. King, King, and Company, Bombay.

Yours most obediently,
J.M.Douie, Acting Chief Secretary,
Government of the Punjab

---

1. Retranslated from the Urdu. The original could not be found. [Publisher]

## *Letter Number 166*[1]

Dated 9th March 1900, Lahore

*FROM:*

> *W.R.H Merk C.S.I, Acting Chief Secretary,*
> *Government of the Punjab*

*To:*

> *Mirza Ghulam Ahmad Sahib, Chief of Qadian,*
> *District Gurdaspur*

Dear Sir! His Excellency Lieutenant-Governor has instructed me to inform you that he sends you his warmest gratitude for your congratulations on the British victories in South Africa.

Yours most obediently,
W. Merk, Acting Chief Secretary,
Government of the Punjab

---

1. Retranslated from the Urdu. The original could not be found. [Publisher]

## *Letter Number 211*[1]

*FROM:*

> *W.R.H Merk C.S.I, Acting Chief Secretary,*
> *Government of the Punjab*

*To:*

> *Mirza Ghulam Ahmad, Chief of Qadian,*
> *Dated 21ˢᵗ March 1900, Lahore*

Dear Sir! I have been instructed to inform you that the British Government of India has accepted with pleasure your congratulations on the British victories secured in South Africa.

> Yours most obediently,
> W. Merk, Acting Chief Secretary,
> Government of the Punjab

---

1. Retranslated from the Urdu. The original could not be found. [Publisher]

## *Letter Number 307,[1] dated 18th April 1900*

LETTER NO. 234:

*Should be dispatched to Mirza Ghulam Ahmad of Qadian Distt: Gurdaspur along with the original receipt dated 26th March 1900.*

AS PER THE DIRECTIVES OF:

*Under Secretary of the Punjab Government*

[Translation of English[1] receipt D. No. 1438]

Lord Mayor fund has been established for the welfare of the wis, orphans, and the wounded of Transvaal. From Bombay on 31st March 1900, an amount of Rupees 500 was received on behalf of Mirza Ghulam Ahmad of Qadian Distt: Gurdaspur and his followers. This donation is intended for the above fund and should be sent to the Right Honourable Lord Mayor in whatever manner appropriate.

Treasurer, King, King, and Company

*Compiled by Mirza Khuda Baksh of Qadian*

---

1. Retranslated from the Urdu. The original could not be found. [Publisher]

# AN ODE

## by Maulawi Abdullah of Kashmir

حمد بیحد مر جناب حضرت پروردگار        آنکه در ہر مظہرے شد حسن رویش آشکار

*All praise belongs to our Lord, the Cherisher and Sustainer,*
*The beauty of whose face shines forth in everything.*

برمظاہر از صفات خویشتن پر تو فگند        بہر تکمیل وجودما بروۓ روزگار

*He made His attributes manifest in things of nature*
*For the perfection of our existence in the world.*

دروجود او و در بقاہم در قیام زندگی        حب حاجت داد ما را جملہ سامان بیشمار

*To ensure our existence, survival, and subsistence,*
*He has provided all necessary means that are countless.*

ہرچہ می بایست مارا بہر جسم ونیز جاں        خود مہیا کرد از رحمت پاٴ ما کردگار

*Everything essential for our body and life,*
*The Lord has provided us out of His mercy.*

خورد و پوش دل پسندو میوہائے خوشگوار آفتاب و ماہ پرویں ایں زمین و آسماں

*The sun, the moon, the stars, this earth and heaven,*

*Exquisite food, clothes and delectable fruit,*

ایں ہمہ گلزار ولالہ آب ہائے آبشار ایں ہوائے خوش کہ ہردم می وزد از لطف او

*This pleasant breeze—blowing each instant by His grace—*

*These gardens, flowers, and spring waters;*

بے عنایا تش زمانہ میشود تاریک و تار ایں ہمہ از رحمت و از لطف ذاتِ کبریا

*All this is due to the grace and mercy of that Supreme Being,*

*Without whose bounties, the world would descend into darkness.*

آنکہ خوبیہائے لطفش ہست بحر بے کنار درحقیقت ہر ثنائے ذاتِ حق رامیبرد

*The True Lord deserves every kind of praise,*

*Whose grace and bounties are a shoreless ocean.*

در مظاہر جلوہ گرشد رحمتش بروزگار از سرِفضل و عنایت حکمت و شان بلند

*On account of His grace, bounty, wisdom, and grandeur,*

*His mercy is apparent in the world by means of His manifestations.*

تاکہ گردد بہر جسم و جان ما او فیض بار از ربوبیت رُخ خود وانمود از مظہرے

*Owing to His Providence, He displays His face through His manifestations,*

*So that our bodies and souls may be blessed with His grace.*

زیں سبب فرزند را مادر گرفتہ در کنار ایں وجود والدیں ظلّے زِ ربّ النّاس ہم

*The existence of parents is also a shadow of the Lord of Mankind,*

*Being the reason why a mother [gently] holds her child by her side.*

برمظاہر کن نظر یاد آر ذاتِ کردگار       از پئے تکمیل اخلاق بشر نکتہ شنو

*For the perfection of human morals, keep this insight in mind;*

*Look at the manifestations of nature and remember that Holy Being.*

از سرِ ایمان من لم یشکر النّاس یاد آر       شکرِ یزداں است شکرِ مظہرِ الطاف او

*Being grateful to the manifestations of His bounties is being grateful to God Himself,*

*And do faithfully bear in mind 'one who does not thank people, [does not truly thank Allah].'*

نیں حقیقت رازِ احساں برجہاں شد آشکار       گفت حق اے مو مناں باوالدین احساں کنید

*The true God says: 'Believers! Show kindness to your parents.'*

*Thus, the secret of His kindness has been revealed to the world.*

از پئے ارواحِ ماشد مظہر پروردگار       رہنمائے دین و توحیدِ خدائے لَم یَزل

*The Guide to Faith and to the Oneness of the Eternal God—[the Holy Prophet*sa*]*

*He became the manifestation of our Lord, the Sustainer for the sake of our souls.*

سر بر آوردہ بعالم چوں خورِ نصف النہار       ایں زماں آں آفتاب از مطلعِ ہندوستاں

*The present age has witnessed that Sun rising from the horizon of India,*

*And shining all over the world like the meridian sun.*

من چہ دانم وصفِ حسن روئے آں عالی تبار       چوں زِ من آید ثنائے آں شہ عالی جناب

*I cannot adequately praise that sublime monarch!*

*How could I grasp the qualities of his handsome face?*

سیّد ما رہبر ما پیشوائے ملک دیں عاشق روئے محمدؐ ہر زماں شوریدہ وار

Our master, our guide and leader of the realm of faith,
An ardent and passionate lover of the face of the Holy Prophet[sa].

می دمد از روئے پاکش بوئے دلدارِ ازل از سرِ گیسوئے مشکینش و زد مُشکِ تتار

His holy face is redolent of the Eternal Beloved,
His scented locks emanate the musk of Tatar.

برجہاں رخشید چوں لیں نیّرِ عالم فروز آبِ حیواں بہر ایماں شد رواں در جوئبار

He shone over the world like a radiant sun,
And the streams ran with life-giving water for the sake of faith.

از نسیمِ نورِ ایماں تازہ شد گلزارِ دل بر دماغِ پاک طبعاں می وزد بادِ بہار

With the fresh breeze of faith, the garden of the heart blossomed.
The spring breeze is blowing over the pure of heart.

در گلستانِ محمد نالہ زد لیں عندلیب باغ دیں ویران گشتہ بازش آوردہ بہار

This nightingale of the garden of Muhammad raised its voice in song,
And brought back spring to the ruined garden of faith.

بلبلے در روضۂ قدس است لیں فرخندہ خو از فغانش قدسیاں را چشم دل شد اشکبار

This blessed person is a nightingale in the garden of purity,
His lamentations have brought tears to the eye of the heart of the
righteous.

درمقام قربِ یزداں پائے او بالا رسید از مَئے عشق محمد شد ز خود بے اختیار

He has ascended high in proximity to God,
And the wine of the love of Muhammad has made him forget himself.

حق بنعمت ہاۓ خویشش درجہاں ممتاز کرد    شد وجیہ درگہ آں عالم ذوالاقتدار

*The true God, through His blessings, set him apart in the world.*

*He was honoured in the court of the sovereign of the world.*

در مقامِ قادیان از آسماں آمد فرود    برزمین مردہ بارید ایں زماں ابر بہار

*He descended from heaven in Qadian,*

*In this age, he emerged forth as the spring rain on dead terrain.*

از پۓ تصدیق او از آسماں آمد ندا    مہر و ماہ ماہِ رمضاں نیز نجم تاجدار

*Heaven spoke in his support,*

*As also the sun, the moon, the month of Ramadan, and the comet.*

عیسیٰ فرخ سیر ہم مہدی آخر زماں    آمدہ از بہرِ تردید خیال کارزار

*The blessed Messiah and Mahdi of the Latter Days*

*Has come to abolish the ideas of warfare.*

ازپۓ سرکوبیٔ ایں غازیان جنگ جو    آنکہ شد اسلام از کردارِ شاں بس شرمسار

*He has come to chastise the [jihadi] warriors,*

*And the ones whose character defames the name of Islam.*

ایں امام وقت آمد تا زِ صدق وراستی    رازِ ایماں برجہانے می نماید آشکار

*The Imam of the Age has come to disclose with truth and veracity,*

*The mystery of faith to the world.*

گفت ملک النّاس در قرآں خداۓ ذوالمنن    ایں اشارہ ہست ظاہر بر وجود شہریار

*The Beneficent God speaks in the Holy Quran of the King of mankind—*

*It is a manifest allusion to the existence of that king.*

در جہاں بہر خلائق بادشاہ دادگر         از عنایاتِ خدا شد ظلّ لطف کردگار

*A king with compassion and high morals*
  *Is a blessing of Allah and a shadow of His mercy*

ہر کہ شکر شاہ عادل رائی آرد بجا         منکر آلائے حق باشد ذلیل و نیز خوار

*Anyone who does not show gratitude towards the just king,*
  *Such a denier of divine blessings ends up humiliated and disgraced.*

آں نبی پاکباز و تاجدارِ انبیاء         عہد کسرٰی را عطا فرمود عزّو افتخار

*That Holy Prophet[sa]—the Crown of Messengers!—*
  *Conferred honour and distinction on the reign of Khosrow.*

نیکوئی بانیکواں فرمودۂ ذاتِ کریم         بدروی سازوبہ نیکاں بدسگال و بدشعار

*The Gracious Lord enjoins us to repay the good with good;*
  *He who repays the good with evil is most vile and depraved.*

حق شناسی فرض باشد بہر مخلوق خدا         کافر آلائے حق ماوائے او بئس القرار

*It is incumbent upon people to recognize the truth.*
  *Those who deny the blessings of the True God end up in an evil place.*

الغرض در عہد پاک ایں شہ ہندوستاں         آنکہ از احسانِ اوبادِ خزاں راشد بہار

*In short, during the holy reign of this king of India,*
  *The fall wind has turned into a spring breeze, thanks to his beneficence.*

ہر طرف گسترد ظلّ معدلت ایں سلطنت         ایں زماں آمد بدنیا نیز مہدی کامگار

*The benign shadow of the justice of this Empire abounds everywhere.*
  *In this very age, the Mahdi—the victorious—has descended upon the*
  *earth.*

هست گورنمنٹ برماسایهٔ یزدانِ پاک          یاد باید کرد عہدِ ظالمانِ نابکار

*This Government is like a merciful shadow of the Holy God,*

*And we must never forget the reign of the evil tyrants.*

ہر کہ وارد عہدِ سکھاں ظلم اوشاں در نظر          تاچہ میکردند جورو ہمتمہا بے شمار

*Whoever witnessed the Sikh rule remembers their tyranny;*

*They had committed countless atrocities.*

آفتے برپا ہمی شد ازپیّے بانگ نماز          ازپیّے یک گاؤ مردم رابسو زندے بنار

*They were prone to create havoc just upon hearing the call for prayers;*

*And to annihilate hundreds of people in retaliation of the slaughter of*

*a single cow.*

از تظلم ہائے شاں دنیا شبے تاریک بود          ناگہاں آمد ز مطلع بادشاہ نور بار

*The world was like a dark night because of their wrongs,*

*Then, all of a sudden, the radiant king made his appearance.*

لیں مبارک سلطنت چوں سایهٔ برماافگند          ناگہاں از لطف حق شدلیل ماشل نہار

*As this auspicious Empire extended its benign rule over us,*

*At once, our night transformed into day by the grace of God.*

شد مہیا امن و دولت از وجود سلطنت          از پیّے ایماں ز بالا نیز آمد شہوار

*Thanks to this Empire, peace and prosperity have been secured,*

*And for the sake of the Faith, a champion has descended from heaven.*

آں خداوندش پیّے اتمام حجت از سما          داد گنجے از معارف نیز تیغِ آبدار

*To clinch the argument, his God has bestowed upon him*

*A treasure of truth and a shining sword from heaven.*

شد مصیر آتھم یک چشم چوں دار البوار      از سنان آسماں دجال اعور را بکشت

*He killed the one-eyed Dajjaal with a heavenly spear,*

*And the one-eyed Aatham, too, landed in Hell.*

آریاں بدسیرزاں روز از حق شرمسار      کشتہ شد از تیغ بّراں لیکھرام بدگہر

*The evil Lekh Raam was also killed with a sharp sword.*

*That day ill-natured Aryas, too, were brought to humiliation by God.*

در وجود مُردۂ آں ایشر بے اختیار      بہر امداد وکیل بدزباں طاقت نہ بود

*The dead, powerless Eeshar[1] was unable*

*To come to the aid of this foul-mouthed advocate.*

باغبانش آب داد شد درخت میوہ دار      ازدرخت روضہ قدس است شاخی ایں جواں

*This youthful champion [the Promised Messiah] is, in fact, a branch of the garden of Paradise.*

*The Gardener Himself watered it and it grew into a fruit laden tree.*

پائے خود را بشکند جانش ہی سوزد بنار      از حماقت میزند ہرکو کہ برپایش تبر

*Anyone who—in his folly—tries to axe this tree down,*

*In reality, cuts his own feet off, and his soul burns in the Fire as well.*

موئے مشکیں بوئے او شد درجہانے عطربار      درجبینش نورِ حق تابد مدام از راستی

*His [the Promised Messiah's] forehead ever shines with the light of truth on account of his righteousness.*

*The aroma of his black locks emanates throughout the world like perfume.*

---

1. Name of God in Hinduism. [Publisher]

در دِلم جوش شد ثنائے آں مہ بدرالدجیٰ لیک درگفتن نیاید شرح بحر بے کنار

*My heart is exuberant with praise for this Full Moon,*

*But it is impossible for me to describe this Shoreless Ocean—*

ایں غلامِ آں شہِ خوباں کہ نامش مصطفیٰ آنکہ از توحید یزداں زد تبر بر پائے دار

*He is the servant of that beloved king whose name is Mustafaa [the Chosen One; i.e. the Holy Prophet[sa]],*

*Who, with the help of Tauheed, demolished the idols lying in the House[of God; i.e. the Ka'bah]—*

کرد ثابت بر جہاں عجزِ بت نصرانیاں میتِ دیرینہ روئے خود نمود از خانیار

*Who has demonstrated to the world the powerlessness of Christian idols,*

*And has shown the long-dead Jesus to be buried in Khanyar [Srinagar].*

عندلیب خوشنوا در روضہ قدس و جلال نالہ زن از عشقِ یزداں آمدہ بر شاخسار

*That melodious nightingale from the garden of holiness and glory,*

*Singing its love for God has come to settle on a lofty bough.*

پہلوانِ آسمانی با کمال عزّ و شاں قدسیاں در خدمت او بر یمین و بر یسار

*That champion of heaven is bestowed with the highest honour and glory,*

*With a retinue of angels attending him on every front.*

کارہائے طاقتِ حق از خدائے وا نمود بردریدہ پردہائے منکریں جیفہ خوار

*Supported by God, he worked wonders to demonstrate the power of truth,*

*And fully exposed the carrion-eating deniers.*

کس بمیدانش نمی آید بروں بهردغا    دشمناں عوعوکنان وجاگزین درکنج غار

*No one comes forward to confront him in public—*
 *The enemies bark like dogs and hide themselves in some dark corner*
 *of a cave.*

بردر و دیوار عالم سخت لرزه اوفتاد    چوں بمیدان وغانک نعرہ زد لیں نامدار

*The whole world shook and quaked*
 *When that prestigious champion raised the battle cry.*

صدر بزم و پیشوا او رہنمائے مؤمنین    ازپئے تائید دین آمد نشانے استوار

*He is the Chief, Imam, and Leader of the Believers,*
 *And [divine] Signs continue to appear in support of Islam.*

از فیوضِ آسماں آراستۂ دارالاماں    شد منور خلق و عالم نیز از گرد و جوار

*The Abode of Peace [Qadian] was adorned with heavenly grace,*
 *And the people, the world [in general], and the environs [of Qadian]—*
 *too—enjoyed illumination.*

از سرصدق وصفا شد خیرخواہ سلطنت    نے بمکر وچاپلوسی بل بحکم کردگار

*He became truly and sincerely a well-wisher of the Government,*
 *Not out of cunning and sycophancy, but under the command of the*
 *Almighty God.*

زانکہ فرمودہ است یزداں نیکوئی بانیکواں    زیں سخن پیچد سرخود جاہل آشفتہ کار

*While God Almighty enjoins us to repay the good with good,*
 *The ignorant and the fanatic turns his back on it.*

جاہل مسجد نشیں برما ملامت می کند        از براۓ خیر خواہی با شہان باوقار

*The ignorant, sitting in the mosque, reproach us,*
  *For showing our goodwill to the glorious kings.*

مانمی ترسیم از غوغاۓ ایں سگ سیرتاں        از نفاق و بدروی داریم شرم و ننگ و عار

*We are not afraid of the barking of these dog-like people,*
  *What we abhor is hypocrisy and bad morals.*

از خدا خواہیم اقبال شہ ہندوستاں        باچنیں ناپاک طبعانِ جہاں ما را چہ کار

*We pray to God for the good-fortune of the King of India,*
  *What have we got to do with these impure, unclean people?*

یا الہ الناس ہر دم جستے باید پناہ        از زیان دشمن جانی کہ باشد مثل مار

*O Lord of mankind, each instant we must seek Your refuge,*
  *Against the danger of that mortal enemy who is like a serpent.*

اے خداۓ ملک و عالم وے پناہ صادقاں        برزمین راست بازاں ابر رحمت را ببار

*O Lord of the realm and the world, and Refuge of the truthful ones!*
  *Make Your cloud of mercy rain down on the earth of the righteous.*

آن خبیثانی کہ پیچیدند از حق روۓ خویش        آتش افشاں برسرشاں بیخ ناپاکاں بر آر

*The wicked who turn away from the truth,*
  *Shall be struck down by a fire that will wipe out the unholy.*

گن نظر برحال زارم از عنایت ہا نواز       از مئے عشق امام عالم مخمور دار

*[Lord] Do attend to my plight and bless me with your favours,*
*And intoxicate me with the wine of the love of the Imam of the world.*

آن مسیح قادیانی عاشق خیر الوریٰ

رحمت حق بر روانش باد اندر ہر دو دار

*That Messiah of Qadian, lover of Best of creation [the Holy Prophet[sa]],*
*May God's mercy envelope him in both the worlds.*

# PUBLISHER'S NOTE

Please note that, in the translation that follows, words given in parentheses ( ) are the words of the Promised Messiah[as]. If any explanatory words or phrases are added by the translators for the purpose of clarification, they are put in square brackets [ ]. Footnotes given by the publisher are marked '[Publisher]'.

To preserve the author's writing style, and particularly his points of emphasis, we have retained his original underlined and bold text styling as well as exclamation marks, including end punctuation for rhetorical questions. However, to facilitate readability for an English speaking audience, punctuation and pauses were inserted as needed, and longer paragraphs were broken into smaller ones.

References to the Holy Quran contain the name of the *surah* [i.e., chapter] followed by a chapter:verse citation, e.g., *Surah al-Jumu'ah*, 62:4, and count *Bismillaahir-Rahmaanir-Raheem* ['In the name of Allah, the Gracious, the Merciful'] as the first verse in every chapter it appears.

The following abbreviations have been used; readers are urged to recite the full salutations when reading the book.

sa *sallallaahu 'alaihi wa sallam,* meaning 'peace and blessings of Allah be upon him', is written after the name of the Holy Prophet Muhammad[sa].

as *'alaihis-salaam,* meaning 'peace be on him', is written after the names of Prophets other than the Holy Prophet Muhammad[sa].

ra *raziyallaahu 'anhu/'anhaa/'anhum,* meaning 'Allah be pleased with him/her/them', is written after the names of the Companions of the Holy Prophet Muhammad[sa] or of the Promised Messiah[as].

rta *rahmatullaah 'alaihi/'alaihaa/'alaihim,* meaning 'Allah shower His mercy upon him/her/them', is written after the names of those deceased pious Muslims who are not Companions of the Holy Prophet Muhammad[sa] or of the Promised Messiah[as].

# GLOSSARY

**Azan** The formal call for Islamic daily Prayers.

**Aameen** A term which literally means, 'so let it be' and is used at the end of a supplication to pray that God may accept it. It is similar in meaning to 'amen'.

**Aryah Samaaj** A Hindu sect founded by Pundit Dayanand in 1875. Their first and foremost belief is that Parmeshwar [God] is not the Creator of matter and souls. Rather, that all of these things are eternal and self-subsisting like Parmeshwar.

**Dajjaal** An Arabic word literally meaning the 'great deceiver'. In Islamic terminology *Dajjaal* refers to those satanic forces which would be unleashed in the Latter Days to oppose the Promised Messiah and Imam Mahdi[as].

**Eid** Literally, 'Happiness that is often renewed'. Eid ul-Fitr marks the end of the month of Ramadan. Eid ul-Adha is celebrated to commemorate Ibrahim's willingness to sacrifice his son for God.

**Fathah** In Arabic script, the vowel mark for 'a' sound, appearing as a diagonal line placed above a letter and designating a short 'a': ‒ if the Arabic letter ا (*alif*) immediately follows, it indicates a long 'a'.

**Hadith** A saying of the Holy Prophet Muhammad[sa]. The plural is *ahaadeeth*.

**Hazrat** A term of respect used to show honour and reverence for a person of established righteousness and piety. The literal meaning is: his/her Holiness, Worship, Eminence, etc. It is also used for God in the superlative sense.

**Holy Prophet**[sa] A title used exclusively for the Founder of Islam, Hazrat Muhammad[sa].

**Holy Quran** The final and perfect Scripture revealed by Allah for the guidance of mankind for all times to come. It was revealed word by word to the Holy Prophet Muhammad[sa] over a period of twenty-three years.

**Iblees** An attributive name meaning 'he turned away'. The Holy Quran reports that Iblis, inflamed by his own arrogance, refused to submit to the Prophet Adam[as].

**Imam Mahdi** A title meaning 'Guided Leader', given to the Reformer of the Latter Days prophesied by the Holy Prophet Muhammad[sa]; *see also* **About Hazrat Mirza Ghulam Ahmad** on page v.

**Jama'aat** Jama'aat means community. Although the word Jama'aat itself may refer to any community, in this book, Jama'aat specifically refers to the Ahmadiyyah Muslim. Jama'aat.

**Ka'bah** The first house built for the worship of God. Located in Mecca. Muslims face Ka'bah while performing their daily prayers and make circuits of it as an act of devotion.

**Khalifah** Caliph is derived from the Arabic word *khalifah*, which means 'successor'. In Islamic terminology, the word righteous *khalifah* is applied to one of the four *Khulafaa'* who continued the mission of Hazrat Muhammad[sa], the Holy Prophet of Islam. Ahmadi Muslims refer to a successor of the Promised Messiah[as] as Khalifatul-Masih. *Khulafaa'* is the plural of *khalifah*.

**Khalifatul-Masih** *see* Khalifah.

**Mahdi** Literally means 'Guided'. *see* Imam Mahdi.

**Maulawi** A Muslim religious cleric.

**Muazzin** A person who calls the *azan* at the appointed times of Prayers.

**Muhammad**[sa] Founder of Islam. *see* Holy Prophet[sa].

**Promised Messiah**[as] A title given to the Reformer prophesied to appear during the Latter Days, by the Holy Prophet Muhammad[sa]; *see also* **About Hazrat Mirza Ghulam Ahmad** on page v.

**Rabb** Lord, Master, Creator; One who sustains and develops; One who brings to perfection by degrees.

**Ramadan** The ninth month of the

lunar calendar of Islam, in which fasting is prescribed for all adult, able-bodied Muslims, except those traveling, ill, pregnant, or nursing.

**Ruboobiyyat** Providence—the quality of sustaining or nurturing.

**Tauheed** The Oneness of God—the fundamental Islamic belief that there is none worthy of worship except Allah.

**Sahib** A title of respect similar to diverse English terms like Mister, Honourable, and Revered.

**Surah** A chapter of the Holy Quran.

**Wali** Literally means 'friend'. In the terminology of Islamic mysticism, it refers to a very pious person or a friend of Allah. The singular form is *wali* [friend] or *waliyyullaah* [friend of Allah], the plural form is *auliyaa'ullaah* which is sometimes abbreviated as *auliyaa'.*

# INDEX

www.ingramcontent.com/pod-product-compliance
Lightning Source LLC
Chambersburg PA
CBHW061050050726
47592CB00004B/1631